Sing to the Lord

DEVOTIONS FOR ADVENT

Sing to the Lord

DEVOTIONS FOR ADVENT

MARY ANNA VIDAKOVICH

UPPER
ROOM BOOKS
Nashville

Sing to the Lord
Devotions for Advent

Cover Design: Cindy Helms
Cover Photograph: Leo de Wys Inc./ Japack
First Printing: August 1994 (5)
Library of Congress Catalog Number: 94-60661
ISBN: 0-8358-0706-1

Printed in the United States of America

For John, Joel, Petra, and Hannah

____Contents____

Introduction

"Hark! The herald angels sing . . ."
"O little town of Bethlehem . . ."
"Silent night! Holy night!"

The Christmas season is a season of singing. People who may not know any other songs, know Christmas carols; people who will not sing any other time will lift their voices to join in the songs of Christmas. This is music that we know and love and songs that we cannot wait to sing.

But wait we must, for it is not Christmas yet. The secular world—with its displays, carols, sales, and Santa—would have us believe that Christmas begins just before Halloween. But the church knows that it is not Christmas yet because we are not ready. We need time to prepare. And we must wait.

The season of Advent, beginning four Sundays before Christmas Day and lasting through Christmas Eve, is the time in which the church waits, watches, and prepares not only for the coming of Christ at Bethlehem but also for the coming again of Christ at the end of time. This season is the reminder that, since the day Jesus ascended into heaven, we have been waiting for his return. Jesus has warned us to be ready. Advent speaks as often of the coming of the Judge in glory as it heralds the coming of the Babe in the manger. It is a season that cannot—must not—be skipped over or rushed through. The waiting during these four weeks is a form of the way we wait for the return of the Lord: with patience and faithfulness, losing sight neither of the goal nor of those around us.

During this Advent season we will examine some of the biblical songs of the coming of the Lord: songs of Isaiah and Mary, Zechariah and Elizabeth, Gabriel and Simeon. Study of the scriptures is an important part of our preparation for Christmas. Here is the foundation for our celebration of God's mighty acts, which will lead to the establishment of the kingdom of heaven. We do not find the whole message of Christmas in the second chapter of Luke or the second chapter of Matthew. The birth of the Messiah is larger than the story of those few days. By expanding our study, we broaden our understanding of the feast for which we are preparing.

An order for daily praise and prayer to use during your devotional time during this study is on pages 11–12. Set aside a few minutes each day to place yourself before God and to prepare yourself for the coming of Christ. Pray slowly the "Call to Praise and Prayer" and the "Prayer of Thanksgiving," giving yourself time to focus on the presence of God. Read the scripture for that day carefully, and spend a few moments in reflection before going on to the written meditation. Then read the meditation and reflect on the meaning it has for you and your life. Some people find it helpful to write their reflections in a journal (noting questions or issues for further reading, meditation, and prayer) and occasionally look back to review the course of their spiritual journey.

Journaling space is provided at the end of each week if you choose to jot down any notes or reflections.

Close with prayer at the end of each day's meditation, the "Personal Prayer"—including prayer for specific people and situations—and the Lord's Prayer. Finally, close with the "Benediction."

An Order of Daily Praise and Prayer

Call to Praise and Prayer

O Lord, open my lips,
and my mouth will declare your praise.
(Psalm 51:15)

****

Prayer of Thanksgiving

New everyday is your love great God of light, and all day long you are working for good in the world. Stir up in us the desire to serve you, to live peacefully with our neighbors, and to devote each day to your Son, our Savior, Jesus Christ the Lord. Amen.

****

Scripture and Reflection

(Use the scripture reading and written reflection for the day. Scriptures are from the New Revised Standard Version.)

****

Personal Prayer

Lord, this day I pray
for the people of my congregation . . .
for those who suffer and those in trouble . . .
for the concerns of our local community . . .
for the world, its peoples and leaders . . .
and for the Church universal—its leaders, members,
*   and mission . . .*
in communion with the saints . . .

****

The Lord's Prayer

(Pray the Lord's Prayer.)

****

Benediction

My Lord, let me go to my appointed place—there to
live and work in the unity of your Holy Spirit, now
and forever. Amen.

****

*

The
First Week
of Advent

** ** ** ** **

_____Sunday_____
Darkness

Scripture: Isaiah 9:2

The Book of Genesis begins with darkness covering the face of the deep. The Exodus from Egypt begins in the darkness of the Passover. The life of Jesus begins in the darkness of the stable. Advent also begins in darkness: the darkness of the world and this present age.

We know the hazards of walking in darkness: tripping and falling over unseen obstacles, wandering off the path and losing our way, being attacked by wild beasts and lawless people. Because we do not know what might be out there, the darkness is something that frightens us.

The darkness of which Isaiah speaks is worse yet. It is not just the outer darkness but also the inner darkness of the spirit; the darkness of those who have lost their way to God. In exile, the people of Israel found their world very dark. They were in a place they knew nothing about and among people who spoke another language and worshiped other gods. Their homes, farms, crafts, and society were gone, and so was the temple—the only place and way they knew to worship God. The Israelites were certain that God had cast them off because of their unfaithfulness and were equally certain that they would never find their way back to God.

It was into this utter despair that God spoke the word of hope: "the people who walked in darkness have seen a great light." We might call this the light at the end of the tunnel. Here is hope that this exile will end, that God will not only take the people back but also will rescue them! This light is like the light of creation shining out over the chaos on the first day of the world.

We, too, live in great darkness. The world around us is a place where evil is real, where life is cheap, where greed is the only guiding principle of the powerful. We feel hopeless and overwhelmed. When Isaiah sings out that on the land of deep darkness a light has shone, we have to know that he means us. The first candle on the Advent wreath is very little light in a world clouded by sin, but it is a beacon of hope, a reminder that God has not left us alone. God is with us, even here! God is with us, even now! The light of the candle is the Light of the Creator. The darkness will not win. Evil will be defeated. The kingdom will come on earth as it is in heaven. Rejoice!

O Lord, Creator of light, keep us safe as we walk in a dark and dangerous world. Help us to move by faith where we cannot see, always clinging to your presence. Let the light of one candle be for us a promise of the Light that is coming into the world, a Light that the darkness will never overcome. In the name of Christ our Light we pray. Amen.

___Monday___
Change

Scripture: Isaiah 9:3-5

The songs of Advent have one recurring theme: things are going to change. When God gets hold of this world, its people, and their institutions, things are going to change. When the kingdom comes, things are going to change! This is the gospel in a nutshell: "The time is fulfilled and the kingdom of God has come near; repent, and believe in the good news" (Mark 1:15)—things are going to change!

How welcome change is depends on where you are in the grand scheme of things. The people of Israel were aching for change. They had been defeated in war and taken into exile as slaves—their cities pillaged and burned, their temple defiled and destroyed, their crops and herds stolen. Isaiah brought them good news. God was going to end their slavery and oppression, and the warfare that had brought them to this place. They would not have to fight their way out; they would only have to follow God.

While this was good news for the Israelites, their captors could not have welcomed it: they were going to lose their slaves and their enemy would be reestablished in Jerusalem without a fight. All that perfectly good warfare for nothing!

We must be careful when we take up the song of Advent that we understand who and where we are. Many of us are not the poorest or most oppressed people of the world. Even those of us in modest circumstances are rich when compared to the majority of people in our world. Even the truly poor among us may live within reach of others who could help. To call ourselves poor or oppressed is to belittle the plight of the millions who know the meaning of those words as we never will.

If we are not the poor or oppressed, are we, then, the oppressors? Although we may have trouble seeing ourselves as oppressors, we have certainly benefited from the oppression of others. Such oppression provides us clothing and cars made by people paid only a few cents an hour, and in some cases, coffee and bananas grown by corporations on land stolen from peasant farmers.

If we are going to join in the rejoicing at the end of oppression, we have to see the big picture, one that depicts God's children everywhere as our brothers and sisters. Join in the charity of this season, but don't limit it to this season only. Things are going to change, beginning with us!

O God of all earth's people, help us to look beyond our enlightened self-interest to truly seek the welfare of our brothers and sisters in all places. Grant that we may see and understand the consequences of our actions, and give us the strength of character and of faith to change in response to the call of the gospel. In Jesus' name we pray. Amen.

___Tuesday___
The Prince of Peace

Scripture: Isaiah 9:6

When God promises change, we expect it to come immediately with flashing lightning and roaring thunder. Yet God almost never chooses to make a spectacle. The light that will come into the darkness is going to come, not with a mighty thunderclap, but with the birth of a child.

Nothing changes the lives of people so radically or immediately as the birth of a child. Parents' lives are turned upside down by this tiny person who requires constant attention and care. The change also affects other members of the family, friends, even strangers. There is something compelling about a new baby that moves nearly everyone to stop, look, and smile. New life has a power in it that speaks to us.

It is not surprising that God chooses a child to bring about the end of war, slavery, and oppression. What would be impossible for an adult is within the grasp of someone so new to the world that he does not yet know what is possible. This is the hope with which we look at nearly every child—that this one might discover the cure for disease, the way to world peace, an end to hunger.

What *is* surprising is the title God gives to this child who is to be born to Israel: Wonderful Counselor, Mighty God, Everlasting Father, Prince of Peace. This is not an ordinary child; this is not even an ordinary royal child, one usually born with many titles. This child will have not only the power but also the name of God. We expect God to come to us in thunder and smoke and fire; we do not expect God to come as a child.

The problems of our world seem to be without solution: governments, police, armies all seem helpless in the face of the evil that people insist on doing to one another. The only solution is in this Child sent by God, the Prince of Peace. Are we willing to align ourselves with this unlikely hero? Are we willing to admit that human strength and wisdom are not enough? Are we willing to let God be God, and then follow where and how this Child leads us? It is not a matter of sitting back and letting God take care of it; it is a matter of following the Wonderful Counselor. We must learn to let go of our self-importance as well as our helplessness and to walk in the way of the Prince of Peace.

O Mighty God, teach us again that our hope for change in the world is not in the strength of any human government or leader or army. Grant that we may acknowledge our helplessness without fear, and rely only upon the saving power of the Prince in whom is the only peace. It is in his name that we pray. Amen.

____Wednesday____
Peace

Scripture: Isaiah 9:7

Peace is one of the main themes of the Advent and Christmas seasons. Peace is central to the God's promises about the coming of the Messiah and the coming of the kingdom. The one who is coming will be the Prince of Peace. God states, "His authority shall grow continually, and there shall be endless peace."

These words have always spoken powerfully to the people of God, perhaps because peace has always been in such short supply in the world. There has not been one single day in the whole history of humankind in which there was not war. Somewhere there is always a nation, a city, a tribe, a clan, or a dynasty doing battle and taking what belongs to someone else. Fighting, strife, and war seem to be facts of human life.

But the one who is coming will bring endless peace for the throne of David and his kingdom. No more war. No more soldiers, weapons, walls, or fortifications. The warriors can go home to their families, build houses, farm the land, tend their flocks, and practice their trades. All of the resources that have been poured into fighting can be turned to the needs of the people. Endless peace!

Notice how this endless peace is brought about: not by destruction of Israel's enemies, nor by making Israel invincible or by transporting Israel out of this world and its troubles. Peace is established and upheld by the Messiah "with justice and with righteousness from this time onward and forevermore." Justice and righteousness are the foundations of peace and the hallmarks of the Messiah's reign.

Often rulers have tried to bring peace through their military might. The so-called "Peace of Rome" began when the emperors ran out of lands to conquer and ended when someone else became powerful enough to conquer Rome. We have been told that peace will come only through superior fire power. Advent reminds us that peace will come when justice and righteousness are practiced from the greatest of rulers to the least of the poor. This is the change that the prophets called for throughout the centuries, a call echoed by John the Baptist. This is the change Jesus preached and taught and lived. Justice and righteousness are not options but are demanded of those saved by God's grace. If we want peace, we must let God change us, and we must let God rule over us.

O God of justice, teach us that the cause of justice and righteousness is not a battle cry with which to arm warriors and justify our hatreds. Help us to open ourselves to the changes you would bring about in our hearts and lives. Grant us the grace to take up the work of justice and righteousness with humility and love. We pray in the name of the One who will establish justice, Jesus Christ our Lord. Amen.

_____Thursday_____
Roots

Scripture: Isaiah 11:1-3

People, like trees, need roots. In a society that is increasingly mobile, we are less likely today than even a generation ago to spend our whole life in one place. We uproot ourselves to go to school, to look for work, and to find a comfortable place to retire. But we need a place to belong, a place to call home, a place that holds our history where we can go back and remember who we are. It may be a town, a family home, a church—each of us needs an anchor for our identity.

The identity of the Messiah is firmly rooted in the history of the people of God. It is unfortunate that the Christian church has so often tried to cut Christ off from these deep Old Testament roots. When we succeed at having a purely "New Testament Christ," we loose the meaning, the power, and the message of God's Messiah.

The stump of Jesse is the royal house of David. God acknowledged and gave permission for the anointing of three kings in Israel: Saul, David, and Solomon. God took the throne away from Saul because of his disobedience and gave it to David and his children. But when Solomon turned to idols and his sons to alliances with foreign powers, God cut off the house of David, leaving only the stump. The promise of the throne to David's offspring continued, waiting only for God to raise up a king who was again worthy to rule over the people. This is the lineage of the Christ: the Messiah is David's son who will be given the throne again. It is much more than a promise to restore the nation; it is a promise that a king will once again rule with God's blessing. Isaiah describes a king whom the people will welcome: wise and understanding, knowledgeable and reverent before the Lord. This is not a tyrant; this is God's own representative, ruling as God would rule.

The roots of the kingdom of God run deep into Israel in the Old Testament. When we wait for the King, we wait for David's son, for a promise made in ancient times. This is not a new thing we are doing, not something recently invented. The King will reign over us as God, renewing the throne that still belongs to the descendants of David. In this season we remember where we have come from, acknowledge our roots, and discover how deep and how ancient they are.

O God of our ancestors, we give you thanks for a history that stretches back through the centuries and embraces those who have been faithful to you in many times and places. We rejoice in the depth of our roots and the nourishment we receive through them. Grant that we may grow and flourish in the strength of all we have been given. In the name of Jesus Christ, son of David and Son of God, we pray. Amen.

___Friday___

Justice

Scripture: Isaiah 11:3-5

Justice is a difficult concept to define because self-interest usually plays some part in the definition. Justice is what vindicates us and those who can help or protect us. If our opponents are vindicated, released, found innocent, and allowed to live, then justice has not been served. We recognize that what we call "the justice system" in our country—police, courts, prisons—functions on this principle of enlightened self-interest: no one is going to do something that will make him or her look bad in the press, cost him or her a coming election, or endanger his or her job. While the system may be still the best we can imagine, there are times when public opinion—not what is truly just—determines the outcome.

This has been the problem with the administration of justice throughout history: people are involved. And people can be influenced, threatened, swayed, bribed, persuaded; people can act to protect themselves and their positions. God promises that the Messiah will come to dispense justice to all the earth and that the Messiah will use a different standard of justice: "with righteousness he shall judge the poor, and decide with equity for the meek of the earth." The real test of justice is not how it is applied to the rich and the powerful, but how it is applied to those who have no power or position in society. Can the poor complain against the rich and receive a fair hearing?

This justice of the Messiah is a frightening prospect because righteousness—the righteousness of God—is the measure of it. We know from the Law, the Prophets, the Gospels how demanding the righteousness of God is on our behavior and conduct. It demands that all have enough, not that we always have some laid aside for a rainy day. It demands that all be cared for, even if they are not like us. It demands that all our business dealings be fair and open and honest, not only to our advantage. The righteousness of God does not allow us to fudge or double-talk; it does not allow us to cheat because we have been cheated; and it forbids us to judge one another. The justice brought by the Messiah gives the poor and the oppressed reason to rejoice; it gives everyone a reason to think hard and look deeply at our normal ways of doing things. What will the Judge say when he comes?

> *O Righteous Judge, grant us the grace to tremble before the prospect of your judgment of us and to confess how far we are from meeting your standard of justice. With the assurance of your forgiveness and your grace, we come before you asking that we might be turned from our sin and self-indulgence to live the Gospel as did Jesus Christ, in whose name we pray. Amen.*

____Saturday____

The Peaceable Kingdom

Scripture: Isaiah 11:6-9

We call the vision described in this passage "The Peaceable Kingdom." It is the place where even the animals are at peace with one another—no longer predator and prey, no longer hunting and eating one another, but all grazing together. We might call it "The Vegetarian Kingdom."

Isaiah uses this vision to illustrate how different the earth will be under the reign of the Messiah. Not only will human relationships be changed by the coming of lasting peace, true justice, and God's righteousness, but even the realm of nature will be transformed so that the order of creation is restored. In the Genesis account of creation, no animal kills or eats another, and none is killed by Adam for food or clothing, until Adam and Eve defy God and are thrown out of Eden. When God kills to make clothing of skins for them, death comes to the animal kingdom as well as to the human. Isaiah speaks of a time when the perfection of Creation will be restored even to the relationships of the animals to humanity and to one another. There will be peace throughout all of the created order.

We tend to look at this beautiful vision without recognizing how difficult, how complete the transformation must be to make it work. For the lion to lie down with the lamb, it is the lion who will have to change. The lion's entire way of life is gone: its diet, habits, instincts, daily activities all are out the window and new ones must be learned. Not to mention acquiring a taste for straw and grass in place of nice, juicy, tender lamb. Poor lion!

Living in the Peaceable Kingdom is going to be very demanding for us, too. Like the lion, we have a lot of changes to make since many parts of our economy are based on war. When we begin to talk about base closings, personnel cutbacks, reduced spending on military hardware, we see how quickly these changes touch us and those around us. We want peace, but we do not want change; we are accustomed to nice, juicy, tender military spending. And we want to be ready to beat up our enemies if they need it—we call it "keeping the peace" as if peace can be brought or kept at the point of a gun. Our sympathies are with the lion, whose jaws must ache as he settles in next to the lamb. And yet, it is the promise of God that this can be done, that we can learn the ways of peace, that even the lion can learn to enjoy alfalfa. This speaks of the power of God to redeem us, to make us right again, to put us into the picture.

> *O God of all creation, we confess to you that we like the way things are, that our lips speak words of peace but our hearts are not ready to change. Remind us of the lion; help us to learn to live in your kingdom without hunger and without fear. In the name of the Lamb of God we pray. Amen.*

Notes and Reflections from Week One

**

The
Second Week
of Advent

** ** ** ** **

_Sunday_____

The Angels' First Song

Scripture: Luke 1:26-29

The songs of the angels begin, not on Christmas Eve with the heavenly host in the skies above Bethlehem, but in Nazareth with the angel Gabriel, who comes to sing the good news for the first time: "The Lord is with you!"

This is not a new song. From the days when Adam and Eve walked with God in the Garden in the cool of the day, through all the encounters of the patriarchs and matriarchs, the warriors, the judges and kings, the priests and the prophets, God has been with the chosen people in many different times and places and ways. It is not even new for the Lord to come to a woman: God was with Sarah, Rachel, Deborah, and Esther, as well as those nameless women whose stories have been lost among the stories of the men of God. Yet, something new and different is about to happen.

"Greetings, favored one! The Lord is with you!" This is the first song of the New Testament, the first song of the fulfillment of all the songs of the Messiah that have come before. Isaiah sang about what the Messiah and his reign would be like; Gabriel sings the coming of the Messiah here and now. The waiting is ending.

We still sing songs about the coming of God's kingdom in much the same words as those of Isaiah. Gabriel reminds us that the day will come when we will hear the song Mary heard, the song that says our waiting has ended and the kingdom has arrived. How will we respond when the angel comes to sing this song to us? Will we, like Mary, wonder what sort of greeting this is—what on earth is this messenger of God talking about? Or have we remembered and sung the songs of Christ's return so that we will recognize and welcome this news?

Mary's world is about to be turned upside down, and it will never be the same again. Both her joy and her pain will be beyond what we can easily imagine. She may well wonder whether it is any favor to be the "favored one."

When angels begin to sing we should look for the world to be turned upside down. Angels never come to proclaim the everyday, only the extraordinary. We watch and wait, for we know neither the time nor the season. We do know that when the Lord is with us again and the kingdom finally comes, everything will be different. All that we think is immovable will be gone; and we, too, shall be changed to be like him.

O God who is with us, help us to keep on singing the songs of the coming of Christ and the establishment of your kingdom on earth. Give us the faith to never lose heart. And remind us to sing with joy for the day we shall see you face to face. In the name of Christ our Lord we pray. Amen.

___Monday___

God's Choice

Scripture: Luke 1:30-33

Gabriel's prophecy must have seemed strange indeed to a young girl of no more than thirteen or fourteen years and still months away from her wedding. She is not a princess nor the daughter of the priest or scribe or someone of position or power. Her fiancé is neither rich nor titled. He is the village carpenter—a good, hardworking craftsman. They are both peasants, the common people looked down on by the Pharisees, taxed by the Romans, and exploited by Herod to build his personal wealth. Gabriel sings of the birth of One who will restore the throne of David, the birth of a king. Surely he is in the wrong house, singing to the wrong girl.

This is almost always our first response to any word God speaks to us: "You must have the wrong number!" We can not believe that God would be able to do anything with us: we are lacking in skill, education, training, background, holiness, time, and proper attire. There are at least a dozen people better qualified to take on the work God has in mind, no matter how large or small it may be. And yet God insists. It may be a call to service in the church or community, a call to deeper relationship with God, a call to more formal ministries in the church, a call to love and service for our neighbors. God insists that this *is* the right number!

Mary is an unlikely choice for God's work, and yet God proposes to do no less than send the Messiah through her. Perhaps she is the perfect choice because anything that happens must be the work of God and not who she is or what she has done. If her son is truly to be the greatest person in all the history of Israel—all the history of the world—it must be by the will and hand of God.

God chooses us to do work in the world for the same reason: we could not possibly do it on our own. If we do anything well—serve on a committee, offer prayer, teach a class, sing in the choir, lead a group, read the lesson, give the sermon, feed the hungry, comfort our neighbors, care for the sick—it is because God is working in and through us, not because we are able to accomplish anything great on our own. All the work is God's work. God brought the Messiah to the world through a simple peasant girl. None of us is asked to take on quite so much, and we are promised that the same God is with us and is still at work.

O Lord our God, we stand before you convinced of our inability to be of service to you. Grant that we may look at your strength rather than at our own weakness, and undertake our work in your name as we rely on you and not on ourselves. In the name of Jesus, who looked to you in all things, we pray. Amen.

____Tuesday____

The Impossible

Scripture: Luke 1:34-37

"For nothing will be impossible with God." If we are able to take only one lesson away from this Advent season, this should be the lesson: "nothing will be impossible with God."

Some things in our lives and our world seem impossible. It seems impossible to solve the economic crisis, to bring peace to those determined to fight, to keep children from starving, to provide health care for the sick, to find housing for the homeless. It seems impossible to find time to pray, to attend a study group, to serve on a committee.

Mary may have been an uneducated peasant girl, but she had a firm understanding of what was and was not possible. And what Gabriel proposed was not possible—except with God. To illustrate this point Gabriel told Mary about her cousin Elizabeth, an old woman six months pregnant with her first child. If Elizabeth could have a son in her old age—when everyone in the family knew she was barren—anything was possible! The mechanics of this conception were less important than the power of God to bring about something so amazing.

We worry a great deal about the mechanics of the impossible. Yet God stubbornly goes on doing the impossible around us every day in defiance of all logic and good sense. "Nothing is impossible with God."

What would happen if we were to let go of reason and logic and deliberately ask God for the impossible? What would happen if we believed, even a little, that

God could make the impossible happen? "You could say to this mulberry tree, 'Be uprooted and planted in the sea,' and it would obey you" (Luke 17:6). There *would* be change—beginning with ourselves and how we see God and the world. The real root of our problem is that we believe that God has little to do with what goes on in the world. Whether because of disinterest or impotence or a lack of desire to be involved, we believe that the *real* world in which we live is somehow removed from the place where God exists. The miracle that Gabriel sang to Mary brought God into the world, and God is still here. There is nothing impossible to God, and therefore nothing impossible—neither peace, nor an end to hunger, nor even a schedule that allows us time before God. It is worthwhile to work toward these ends, to have these goals because nothing is impossible!

> *O God of the impossible, help our unbelief! Teach us to seek you in all things and not just in those things that we think are possible. Remind us that you are interested and involved, and you are still creating in our world. We lift to you all of the impossible problems we face, and pray in the name of Jesus Christ our Savior, who performed miracles in your name. Amen.*

_____Wednesday_____
The Servant of the Lord

Scripture: Luke 1:38

Few people have the confidence to sing by themselves. It is one thing to sing in a group—the larger the better—but when the other voices begin to fade away, most of us fall silent. It takes time, practice, and self-confidence to learn to sing alone. One thing the angel Gabriel taught Mary was how to sing. We do not know whether any of these passages we now call canticles or songs, was sung to music as we sing hymns. They are called songs because they are more than just spoken words—more beautiful, more profound, more important. Mary speaks her questions to Gabriel, but in this final verse she sings her reply to all that God has said to her: "Here am I, the servant of the Lord; let it be with me according to your word." Mary's faith and willingness to do what God has asked of her causes her reply to sing.

When we say, "It is God's will," often we are speaking of a situation that we feel is beyond our control, beyond hope. Unlike Mary, we do not sing the words. Perhaps it is because we do not know whether what has happened is God's will or simply the result of human frailty. So we keep the situation at arm's length by putting it on God's shoulders. What if we embraced God's will for us as Mary did—willingly, singingly? It would certainly change the way we see these situations. Instead of seeing only tragedy and hopelessness, we would proclaim God's purpose, calling, tasks to be done and life to be lived. We might even learn to sing.

Mary could have seen what was about to happen as a tragedy. It certainly must have given her some difficult days as she explained all these things to her parents and to Joseph and as she endured the pointing and gossiping of neighbors and the nosy questions of family members. Yet Mary believed in the goodness of God and willingly embraced the plan. There is both humility and great faith in her response: "Here am I."

When God wants to do great things with us, through us, and around us, do we stand up and sing, "Here am I"; or do we hide under the bed until God goes away? If we believe that God can do all that has been foretold to bring the kingdom of heaven on earth, then we must learn to answer, "Here I am, the servant of the Lord." God's work still requires human hands and feet, human hearts and minds, and our voices lifted up in song.

> *O God of music and song, teach us to sing. We are surrounded by a world that witnesses to your goodness and grace—the birds in the air, the lilies in the field, even the pastures in the wilderness. When you call us, teach us to answer, "Here am I" so that we may be channels of your goodness and grace. We pray in the name of our Lord Jesus Christ. Amen.*

___Thursday___
Elizabeth

Sc.ipture: Luke 1:39-45

Mary is not the only one who has learned to sing. Her cousin Elizabeth, the wife of Zechariah the priest, is pregnant in her old age in accordance with God's word to Zechariah. In that society, to be childless was to be not only without heirs or support in old age but also was considered a sign of God's displeasure. Elizabeth certainly had something to sing about now before her family and neighbors who had pitied, ridiculed, and judged her.

But that is not the reason she sings. Elizabeth's song is not about herself or her good fortune or even about what God has done for her. She is filled with the Holy Spirit and begins to sing about what God has done for Mary. Elizabeth recognizes immediately the work of God, and Mary's willingness to take part in it. She blesses Mary because Mary has "believed that there would be a fulfillment of what was spoken to her by the Lord" (Luke 1:45).

How easy it is to recognize the work of God! We know when we look at certain people such as Mother Teresa in the streets of Calcutta or Bill Kreeb at Neighborhood House in East St. Louis, that they are filled with the Spirit, doing the work of God. Just to see these saints at work is to recognize God at work—the Spirit within us recognizes the Spirit within them. The life of faith is a witness and a source of strength. By living faithfully we strengthen one another, making it possible for the whole church to sing praise to God. Our faithfulness is not just between ourselves and God—it reaches out to touch all those around us who are trying to live faithful lives.

Mary and Elizabeth, by doing what the Lord had asked, strengthened and inspired each other. Their time together prepared Mary to face the people of Nazareth, and prepared Elizabeth for the hardships of raising a son who would become a prophet. The fellowship of Christians who are doing the will of God in their own lives and in the world is important. We need to be strengthened by one another's presence, witness, and love; we need to feel the Spirit in us respond to the Spirit in others in songs of praise and thanksgiving to God. There is no solitary Christian. We need one another—whether we are old or young, Mary or Elizabeth—if we are to do the will of God.

> *O God of us all, help us to recognize the work you are doing in and through those around us. Help us to be transparent, that others may see the strength and grace that the Holy Spirit pours into us day by day. We pray in the name of Jesus, in whom all humankind sees you at work. Amen.*

____Friday____
The Model of Discipleship

Scripture: Luke 1:46-49

The church has long debated what it wants to say about Mary, the mother of Jesus. Over the centuries it has gone from one extreme to the other, sometimes revering Mary to the point of worship and other times ignoring her. Protestants have difficulty with Mary. We tend keep her in the Christmas story and ignore her the rest of the time. Yet Mary is the point on which the whole gospel story turns. It is Mary who said, "Yes," to God, Mary who became the human agent in the plan of salvation. It is Mary who tells us who she is, how she fits in, and why, as she sings her song of praise, which we call "The Magnificat." Without her there is no Bethlehem, no cross, no empty tomb.

All of Mary's attention, praise, and worship is focused on God her Savior. She never allows us to think that she is anything but the servant of the Lord. When she speaks of the generations to come who will look at her and say that she was truly blessed, it is not because of what she has done but rather because "the Mighty One has done great things for me." Mary always maintains that it is God's actions that must be praised, and not her—all she has done was to be obedient.

Mary is the first disciple of Jesus, present at every critical moment of his life. She is the first and best witness about many of the events of his life, and must have been an important source of information for those who recorded the Gospels. Because she so perfectly models the life of a person of God, we cannot—must not—dismiss her. It took great courage for Mary to live the life to which God called her. And she lives it faithfully, always pointing away from herself to God who has done great things for her and to Jesus, the Messiah, who has come to speak God's Word to humankind.

This is the model of discipleship: to point away from ourselves and call people's attention to the work of God and the life of Christ. This is not easy for us; we are not well schooled in deflecting the credit. Our society values only those it can hold up, recognize, write stories about, and photograph. To be like Mary is to pass unnoticed singing of what God has done rather than our own praises. It is not weakness but strength that Mary shows us. She is indeed blessed because she has shown us the life of discipleship to which we are also called.

O Mighty One, grant that we may always keep in mind the life and example of Mary as we strive to live faithful lives. Teach us to sing with her the songs that praise what you have done, what you are doing, what you will do with us and in us and for us. In the name of Jesus Christ, the Son of God and son of Mary, we pray. Amen.

_____Saturday_____

God's Attention Span

Scripture: Luke 1:50

One thing that Mary—as the prophets and psalmists before her—understood was that God's attention is lasting. This is hard for us to imagine. We have incredibly short attention spans, lasting only from one crisis to the next. What were the issues in the political arena last February? Where was the *hot* war, famine, disaster? It is hard to remember because we are caught up in the issues, wars, and disasters of the moment. Next month we will have forgotten these and gone on to something new. When we cannot pay attention, cannot remember any longer than this, how can we imagine a God who pays attention, who remembers, and who is faithful not just for a month or a year but from generation to generation?

The essence of Mary's praise for God is that God has remembered the faithful people over the centuries, over the millennia. God remembered the days of Miriam and Moses, the days of Abraham and Sarah, and even the days of Adam and Eve. God has never forgotten the promises made to the people, has never failed to show mercy to all of those who have come in the long march of years since those promises were made. How astounding! The promises made in a different time and a different place to people no longer alive are now being fulfilled in Mary as she cooperates with God to bring the Messiah into the world.

We stand heirs to another set of promises made long ago in a different place to different people long dead: the promise that Christ will return, that the kingdom of God will be established on the earth, and that the reign of God over all creation will be restored. But with our short attention span, we have trouble remembering these promises. At best, they are vague images of the end of the world; at worst, meaningless words which someone obviously misunderstood somewhere along the way. It is not happening now, so we do not take time to worry about it. But God remembers. And God is faithful. Just as the promise of the Messiah was kept in Mary's lifetime, the promise of his return will be kept.

Mary's proclamation of the faithfulness of God is a wake-up call for us: God's promise will be kept. It falls to us to be prepared for the day of Christ's return, to be working with the vision of the kingdom before us in order to speed the day when it is, at last, fully come. God's mercy continues from generation to generation, including ours.

> *O God of all history, help us to see the big picture—the whole sweep of time with which you are concerned—and to see our place in it. We are not the first or the greatest; we may not be the last. But we thank you that, even if we are the least, you still remember us and that your promises, your grace, your mercy are for us too. In the name of Jesus Christ, the faithful one, we pray. Amen.*

Notes and Reflections from Week Two

***

The

Third Week

of Advent

** ** ** ** **

_____Sunday_____
Mary—the Prophet

Scripture: Luke 1:51-53

It is important to remember who Mary is as she sings her song. She is a peasant, someone without wealth, power, or position. She is a woman and women in her society had no rights. As a woman she lacks the right to speak on any subject and is at the mercy of the men in her family who make all decisions for her. Mary is a person who lives under the conquering army of Rome and the corrupt rule of Rome's puppet king, Herod the Great. She understands what it means to be oppressed, starved, and held captive. Mary stands with the prophets as she takes the side of those who are like her and sings of what God is doing: God is preparing to turn the world upside down.

Like Isaiah, Mary tells us that things are not going to continue as they are now. When God accomplishes this business of sending the Messiah and redeeming the world, things will be so different that we may have trouble recognizing them. The comfortable will be afflicted and the afflicted will be comfortable.

This is where we object—especially if we are reasonably comfortable—and say that it makes no sense for everyone to switch places. Even then there will still be the comfortable and the afflicted, the oppressors and the oppressed. If only the identities change, then the real state of things will not have improved. And this is true. If God is just going to move the place cards and leave the basic order of things the same, the result will be as unjust as what we have now.

The world that Mary and the prophets sang about, in which the kingdom of God has been established, is much more complicated. It is a place where there is equity, where everyone has enough, where resources of every kind are shared rather than hoarded or sold. It is a place where there is no ladder, no "haves" and "have nots." To get there, the proud and powerful and rich will have to give up their control, will have to be brought lower; and the hungry and lowly will have to be raised up and given some of what they have not had before. It is not a matter of changing places but of bringing everyone to the same level, which will be higher for those like Mary and lower for those like Herod—a place where we all can look one another in the eye. Mary sings about it; Herod rages. We are called to join in the songs.

O God from whom all blessings flow, help those of us who have been blessed with material wealth to heed your call to step down from our superior positions while we reach out to lift up those who live in poverty and want. Remind us that there is a place at the table for all of your children to sit side-by-side. We pray in the name of Jesus Christ, brother of us all. Amen.

____Monday____
The Story of Salvation

Scripture: Luke 1:54-55

The end of Mary's song reminds us that the story of salvation about which she is singing is nothing new: it has a long history with deep roots in the story of Israel, and goes back even to the story of the Creation.

The retelling of this story is essential to knowing who we are as people of God. We tend to be so poorly versed in our own personal histories that the longer history we share is hard for us to grasp.

In recent years there has been a renewed interest in genealogy, and many families have searched to find their familial roots. While some have traced certain branches of their families back a dozen or more generations, it is difficult for most of us to reach back to the time before our ancestors arrived in North America. A genealogy of six or seven generations is a prize.

The children of Israel never failed to keep track of the family tree. Every Passover they would gather to tell again the stories of how God brought them out of slavery in Egypt and gave to them the Promised Land. This history stretches back to the dawn of civilization—to wandering Arameans named Abraham and Sarah, to a boat-builder named Noah and his family, to gardeners named Adam and Eve.

All of this is our history as well. It is the story of our salvation. We cannot begin with Easter Sunday or Good Friday, the day of Jesus' baptism in the Jordan, or Christmas Eve. If we want to tell the story we have to go all the way back and start at the beginning. To recall this sweep of history reminds us that our story is the story of the people of God, not only of individuals. Because the promise was made to "Abraham and his descendants forever," we stand in the line of salvation. We are a part of something much larger than ourselves, something that will continue after our bodies have returned to the dust from which Adam and Eve were made.

Mary ends her song by giving us a glimpse of the story of salvation, beginning with her ancestors and continuing through uncounted generations that she cannot number or imagine. We stand in a great company—the people of God—taking up the song of all that God has done. It is not a song of what God has done for me alone, but what God has done for all of us in the great train of the faithful that stretches to eternity.

O Lord, Eternal God, we thank you for all who have gone before us and for the witness to your presence, your goodness, and your faithfulness that they have left for us. Grant that we may remain faithful, and may add our witness to theirs as we pass it on to the generations of your people who are yet to come. In the name of Jesus our Savior we pray. Amen.

Tuesday

Joseph's Dance

Scripture: Matthew 1:18-23

It is not surprising to hear an angel sing at this point in the story. The angels have sung to Zechariah and to Mary already and are beginning to tune up for the chorus over Bethlehem. What is surprising is that we do *not* hear Joseph singing: Not only do we not hear Joseph sing, we do not even hear him speak in all of the Gospel record of the birth and life of Jesus. This silence has relegated Joseph to the back of the manger scene and the lead rope of the donkey, little more than window dressing in the Christmas story. If we look closely, however, we see that Joseph's song is not one of words or music, but it is a powerful dance of deeds and action.

Joseph is an honest, hardworking carpenter in the village of Nazareth. Although he is not a member of any of the religious factions, he is faithful in his religious observance. When Mary comes to tell him that she is pregnant, he knows that the Law would permit him to have her executed. But he chooses instead to divorce her quietly and minimize the scandal for both of them. Joseph has already begun the dance of one who deals thoughtfully with the reverses of life—a skill he will need.

When the angel explains the situation to Joseph and asks him to go through with the wedding—to become foster father to this child who will be Emmanuel, "God with us"—Joseph does not ask a lot of questions—as Mary did—or disbelieve that this is possible or true—as Zechariah did. As far as the records show, he says nothing. Joseph acts; he does what the angel has asked.

We tend not to value dance as highly as we do song. It is much more difficult for us to understand, and much more difficult for most of us to do. In singing, there are words that we can write down and read off and sing along when the right music is played. But to dance requires that we watch closely, and then convince our bodies to duplicate the motions. Even if there are footsteps on the floor to follow, we still have arms and heads to guide as well.

Joseph is an example of how important it is to learn to dance with God. It is his ability to dance—to follow where God directs—that allows Joseph to keep his family safe and to raise Jesus to strong, intelligent adulthood. To be a disciple is to dance with God, to follow with deeds and actions the direction that God is giving us. Let us join in the Advent music with Joseph, the dancer.

O Lord of the Dance, we cannot just stand and listen when you speak to us; it is not even enough for us to stand in the back of the chorus and sing the right words. Teach us how to dance the dance of discipleship, following with our lives the deeds and actions of our Lord Jesus Christ, who lived the dance, and in whose name we pray. Amen.

____Wednesday____
Zechariah

Scripture: Luke 1:67-68

Who? Zechariah? Even those who have read and reread the New Testament can be excused for failure to immediately place Zechariah: he is not one of the main characters in the story. Zechariah is, however, one of the singers, and his song is an important part of Advent. Zechariah, a priest of the order of Abijah, was a righteous man who had lived a long and—Luke tells us—blameless life. One day as he was offering incense in the sanctuary of the Lord, an angel came to tell him that he would be the father of a prophet on whom the spirit and power of Elijah would rest. Being an old man with an equally old, and barren wife, Zechariah doubted the angel. As proof, the angel struck Zechariah mute until the birth of his son.

When John, later called the Baptist, was born, Zechariah's voice returned. Since Zechariah knew that God was working out the salvation of the people before his very eyes, the first thing he did was sing. If his son was to be the one "to make ready a people prepared for the Lord" (Luke 1:17), then the Lord could not be far behind.

If God were to strike mute all of those who doubt—or worse yet, laugh—when God speaks a word to them, the world would be a very quiet place. Even those who faithfully serve the Lord, as Zechariah did, for some reason have difficulty believing that God is actually going to do something here and now. We may not doubt God's ability to do miraculous things, to change people and situations; we just do not believe that it will happen somewhere as ordinary as where we are, or with people as ordinary as those who surround us.

Perhaps it would be good if we had to stay quiet and watch what God was doing around us. Once God manages to get our attention, we might be amazed to see all of the miracles taking place. Finding our voices again, we, too, might be ready to say, "Blessed be the Lord God of Israel!" Zechariah found faith during his silence, discovering that he could really believe all of the words he had said over the years as he carried the people's needs and prayers to God. He was now able to see in his small son the evidence that the redemption of the people had already begun in the coming of the Lord's messenger. Do we see around us every day the work of preparing the way for the kingdom of God?

> *O God of wonders, as we look around us it is hard for us to recognize in this place and these people a stage for your mighty work. Help us to be silent and watch what you are doing all around us. Then give us voice to rejoice in all that you have done; to no longer say "luck" or "coincidence" or "unknown cause," but instead to say, "The hand of the living God!" We pray in the name of Jesus, who brought silence to the storm. Amen.*

____Thursday____

Enemies

Scripture: Luke 1:69-71

David was the first and only king to rule Israel in peace and security. It was David who finished the work of conquering the Promised Land and who took possession of all that God had promised to Abraham. David conquered Jerusalem and established his capital there, bringing the Ark of the Covenant—and so the presence of God—to dwell in what has since been called the Holy City. During the reign of David, Israel was a power to be reckoned with. Things began to unravel, however, during the time of David's son, Solomon; and when Solomon died the kingdom was divided and David's throne left empty. Enemies continued to descend upon Israel and Judah, and the land was always in a state of upheaval. What greater hope could the people have than that they will be delivered from the hands of their enemies and those who hate them? What better work could a redeemer do? With the return of David's heir, the enemies will be cast out.

Zechariah, living under the rule of the latest conquerors, understood how important this hope was for the people: the need for salvation from the Romans was keenly felt.

We do not feel our need for salvation as immediately as did Zechariah. When we identify our enemies, they are rarely people who have much real power over us. Our political enemies are those with whom we disagree on any number of points, but unless we rely on political patronage jobs for our livelihood, these people have only the power to raise our blood pressure.

Personal enemies may occasionally put us in real danger—a fact becoming more common in our current state of easy violence—but most of the time these are people we avoid rather than fear.

Our real enemies, those from whom we need to be rescued by the Mighty Savior, are sins rather than people: greed, oppression, lethargy, exploitation, prejudice, apathy, pride, self-satisfaction. These attack the people of God, though we may lack any human enemy or physical danger. We will not feel the urgent need of a Savior until we recognize that we still are surrounded by the enemy and will surely be defeated without help. We are in deep trouble; but God is acting to save even us.

> *O God, our Rock and our Redeemer, keep us ever mindful of our need to be saved from all of our enemies, and most particularly, from our sins. Keep us from becoming blind to our own faults and failings which prevent our living the gospel as you have called us to do. Keep us also from despair, for we have a Savior in Jesus Christ, and we pray in his name. Amen.*

____Friday____
Life without Enemies

Scripture: Luke 1:72-74

What would it mean for us to be free of our enemies? This is a question that has been asked by many people in these days that follow the end of the Cold War. We have lived so long—some of us all of our lives—knowing who and where the enemy was. We have believed that without our constant vigilance and preparation, the Soviet Union would destroy us in a moment.

So, we must answer the question: What does it mean to be free of our enemies? Must we devise new rivalries in order to have a focus for our fears? Or is it possible for us to find a new way to live in peace?

At first glance this may appear to be a political question. It is actually a theological one. God has shown mercy, remembered the covenant with our ancestors, and rescued us from our enemies—now what? Do we rush back into the situation from which God has lifted us? Or do we learn to live in this new situation, this place of redemption? It will not be easy because we will have no one to blame for our troubles but ourselves. And we will have to learn to give God all the attention we had focused on our enemies. It is easier to watch other people who expect the worst of us than to constantly look into the face of the Almighty, who expects the best of us. With no enemies we have to learn to act better—with one another as well as with those in other places. We too have to learn to see all human beings as children of God and act accordingly. We have to tenderize ourselves, shedding the hard shell of indifference that enmity always requires. This is going to be uncomfortable.

What will we do without enemies? We will work very hard to live faithfully before God.

O Lord, God of all the nations, teach us how to live without enemies. Show us how to trust rather than fear, how to lift up rather than trample down, how to build rather than destroy. Help us to learn to be courageous in new ways, to risk ourselves in life rather than in death. It is in the name of the Prince of Peace, Jesus Christ our Lord that we pray. Amen.

___Saturday___
Freedom

Scripture: Luke 1:74-75

When we talk about freedom, we tend to speak in terms of what we have earned, won, protected, and established. We see our political freedom as the result of our efforts and our vigilance, and we assert that it is ours to do with as we please. Many of the struggles we face today are the struggles over what we are free to do— with or without one another's consent.

Zechariah is singing about a different kind of freedom. This is not freedom to do whatever we want; it is freedom to serve God "without fear, in holiness and righteousness . . . all our days." God frees us for a reason, frees us to do something in particular. Something in us rebels against this kind of freedom. If we are freed only to serve God, that may seem to us just another kind of slavery, even if it is benevolent.

Zechariah, however, saw service to God as the highest freedom. Because of his position as a member of the priestly order of Abijah, he was periodically freed from his usual work and obligations so that he could go to the temple to serve God at the altar. Freedom from the rule of Rome would mean that all the people could order their lives once again around God and God's law. They would be free to come to the temple and worship without fear.

We are very much in need of this kind of freedom. "Oh," we say, "but we *have* freedom of religion!" Indeed. What we need is not political or constitutional or legal freedom; we have those. We need freedom to worship God in holiness and righteousness all our days. This is an interior freedom. We are so bound by the expectations of society, the opinions of those around us, the requirements of the *good life*, the American Dream, that we lack the freedom to worship God as God would have us worship: not just one hour on Sunday or a few minutes a day, but with every moment and every act of our lives. This is freedom not just to say, "This society has its values backwards," but to live our lives upside down in relation to the rest of society because this is the way Jesus commanded us to live. This is the freedom to reject the accepted definitions of success—fame, fortune, the American Dream—so that we may live a holy and righteous life in harmony with God.

We need to be set free! Even when we can see what it means to live that way, even when we truly comprehend the gospel and accept its demands on our lives, we must look to God to set us free to actually live it all our days, in all our ways.

> *O Lord God, set us free from Madison Avenue, from Hollywood, from Wall Street; set us free from the Joneses; set us free from our own fear of being different in a society that expects us all to dream one Dream. Set us free to live before you lives becoming the Gospel, lives proclaiming the Gospel. We pray in the name of Jesus Christ, who has shown us how to live. Amen.*

Notes and Reflections from Week Three

****

The

Fourth Week

of Advent

** ** ** ** **

_____Sunday_____
Preparation

Scripture: Luke 1:76

We are deep in the work of preparing for Christmas: decorations, cards, worship, parties, holiday gatherings, gifts. We work so hard to get ready for Christmas that it is no wonder most of us collapse in a heap on December 26! It is hard work to get everything ready.

Zechariah knew that his son, John, would be the one who would do the work of preparing the way for the Messiah, and that this would be no small task. Israel had not had a prophet for over 200 years, but John would have to be a "prophet of the Most High" if he was to get the people ready. Isaiah compares this task to building a highway through the desert, a difficult enough job with all of our modern technology and transportation; the work of a lifetime—or more—in the ancient world.

Even though the coming of the Messiah had been promised and prophesied for centuries, and even though the people longed for the coming of God to deliver them, no one was ready. Few people, from chief priest to lowliest slave, understood how the Messiah would come or who he would be. They pictured a warrior king like David who would take control of the political and military situation or a prophet like Moses who would intervene and dramatically deliver the people. And they expected Elijah, the forerunner of the Messiah, to return the way Elisha had seen him go: in a chariot of fire from heaven. If Jesus was not the Messiah they expected, neither was John the prophet they had envisioned. John came, not with flash and thunder but with a pick and a shovel to begin building a road in the desert. John had to be an extraordinary person because he was called to extraordinary work.

The most important preparation for Christmas is one that will not go on a wall, a door, a table, or under the tree. The most important preparation for Christmas is still the building of the road through the desert, the preparation in our spiritually barren world of a way for the Lord to walk. How do all of our more usual preparations make a way for the Lord? Do we witness to the secular holiday or are we preparing for the Holy Day of God's coming? We do not have to outlaw Christmas to recapture its holiness; we just have to remember our goal. We want this road to go straight to God in praise and thanksgiving.

> *O Lord, help us to stay focused on the reason for all of this activity and celebration. Grant that we may move just slowly enough through the rush of activity to keep the birth of the Savior at the center of our giving, our greetings, our rejoicing. Help us to be road builders in the good company of John the Baptist, making the world ready for Christ, in whose name we pray. Amen.*

___Monday___

Forgiveness

Scripture: Luke 1:77

One thing is absolutely necessary for a person to be forgiven: that person has to believe that he or she has done something wrong, something for which he or she needs forgiveness. This is the largest obstacle to reconciliation on any level: between family members, friends, nations, humanity, and God.

John the Baptist will bring the gospel, the good news of salvation, to the people of Israel. But first he must convince them that they need to be saved, that they have sins that need to be forgiven. Building a highway through the desert with bare hands is a piece of cake by comparison! This is why John the Baptist is such a fearsome presence in the scriptures: it is not that he does not understand God's love, but that he must get these people ready to accept that love when it comes, and so he must convict them of their sin. He will also give them the remedy for sin, first in baptism for forgiveness, and then in his witness to the Messiah who is coming after him with God's salvation.

We all readily agree that God forgives sin, that Jesus brought salvation from sin, but we have a very hard time seeing ourselves as those who need forgiveness and salvation. We watch the evening news or read the newspaper and decide that we really are not so bad after all; the things we may have done—*may* have done!—are not anything compared to what other people are doing. We are angels by comparison, and surely God must look on us with pleasure when God sees how bad everyone else is. Instead of regretting and repenting of our sins, we feel good because we stack up so well in the comparison. In *Answering God: The Psalms as Tools for Prayer*, Eugene Peterson writes, "Most of the sins that we do not commit are not because of our virtue, but because we lack either energy or opportunity." We will never have an accurate picture of ourselves and our fallen human condition until we understand that there is no sin we are incapable of committing. We are indeed sin-filled and without hope of ever being any better on our own; "not that bad" is certainly bad enough in comparison to the righteousness of God, which is the only comparison that matters.

Zechariah sings out the good news that first his son and then the Messiah will declare: God has come to bring the people knowledge of salvation by the forgiveness of their sins. We are forgiven as soon as we grasp the fact that we need forgiveness. Having no righteousness of our own, we are given the righteousness of God as a gift of salvation: the first and best Christmas present.

> *Loving God, out of your goodness you are ready to forgive us. Help us to accept that we need to be forgiven. Grant that we may see ourselves as we are, that we may recognize our faults and failings, and may come to you with true and heartfelt repentance. And when we are ready, we pray that you will speak to us the words of forgiveness. In the name of Jesus Christ we pray. Amen.*

_____Tuesday_____

The Hints of Dawn

Scripture: Luke 1:78-79

Zechariah ends his song—and his appearance in the scriptures—by echoing the songs of the prophets who have gone before him, particularly the songs of Isaiah with his images of light and peace. Zechariah stands only six months from the birth of the Messiah at Bethlehem, and he can already see the first light of the dawn of God's coming; he sings because he sees the day that has been promised.

This must be what it would have been like to watch the first day of the Creation: out of the swirling darkness God calls for light, and everything is changed in an instant. With light all manner of things are now possible, including the making of the world and the life of all things that will grow and live upon it.

Paul reminds us that salvation is not just for humanity but for everything God made, everything that has been so twisted and deformed by the sin of human beings (Rom. 8:18-24). Thus, God's light breaking into the world through the Messiah is the dawn of a new creation. It is the restoration of everything God created. The shadow of death will vanish in the brightness of the light of God that is coming, and we will be guided again into the ways of peace. The end of war and death signal the end of sin and brokenness.

The early Christians watched eagerly for the dawn of the Day of the Lord, for the light in the sky that would signal the return of Christ. Over the centuries, however, many have stopped looking, stopped expecting. Peter even speaks of scoffers who will come asking, "Where is the promise of his coming?" (II Peter 3:4). While we do well to listen to Jesus' warning not to be led astray by those who come saying, "I am he!" (Luke 21:8), we are unprepared to recognize the dawn when it comes.

The church needs to learn again the urgency of living in the last days, to be ready to greet the Lord at the end of time. It is not a matter of selling everything and moving to the mountains. Rather it is living as if the day has already come, and God has begun to remake the world in God's own image with us as partners in the work. Then we will be in the light, following Jesus in the paths of peace.

> *O God our Creator, give us the vision of Zechariah that we may see that the first hints of dawn are already on the horizon and that your kingdom is about to break forth on the earth. Grant that we may hear your call to join in the work of creation. Lead us and guide us as we set our feet on the path of peace. We pray in the name of Jesus, the Light of the World. Amen.*

____Wednesday____
John the Baptist

Scripture: Luke 3:15-17

John the Baptist strikes a sour note in the midst of our Advent singing. We have listened to angels sing of God's promises being fulfilled and to faithful mortals sing of their obedience to God. Into this uplifting chorus comes the harsh voice of the Baptist singing out a warning of the judgment that is about to come, of One who is coming with the Holy Spirit and fire.

Wait a minute! There is no room in the manger scene for the Holy Spirit and fire! All we have room for is a cute little baby surrounded by gentle animals, and adoring parents, shepherds, and kings. We have separated the birth of Jesus from the rest of his life. We fail to see in the manger the One who will teach and heal and die on a cross. We need the song of John the Baptist in Advent to remind us of who is being born, who is coming to us.

It is easy to see the coming of the Messiah into the world as an event only surrounded with peace and well-being. Such an event should make no demands on us as we join in the chorus of heaven and earth. But the prophets speak of this day as the day of judgment, "the great and terrible day of the Lord" (Joel 2:31), and the people are warned to prepare for it.

John reminds us who we are as we await the coming of the Savior: we are a people in need of salvation. We are not a righteous and holy band come out to greet the Messiah as equals. We must be saved by his grace, or we will be burned with the chaff of the threshing floor. We make the birth of Christ nothing when we act as if we do not need a Savior. If we know we must cling to the cross, there is all the more reason we should cling to the manger with tears and prayers, as this is the place God's grace enters our world—the Incarnate God begins the last chapter in the work of salvation. Without the cradle there is no cross, no salvation, and only the fire that destroys the chaff.

John sings to remind us of why we are here: to receive the Holy Spirit and the baptism of fire. We should tremble in our shoes because, like John, we are met by One we are not worthy to serve. And yet it is a song of hope, because the fire that comes in Christ does not bring destruction, but light and life and the renewal of all things.

O Lord our God, save us from coming too easily and with too much self-assurance to the birth of our Savior. Remind us that we stand in need of salvation, and that salvation begins with the baby in the manger. Grant that as we approach him there, we may come humbly and thankfully, knowing that he brings in his tiny life all that is necessary for our salvation. We pray in the name of our Savior Jesus Christ. Amen.

_____*Thursday*_____
Simeon the Prophet

Scripture: Luke 2:25-30

We tend to believe that the Holy Spirit did not become active in the world and the community of faith until the Day of Pentecost. But in the first two chapters of Luke we see the Holy Spirit filling and moving to *song* people who would otherwise be very minor characters in the story, if we noticed them at all. Elizabeth, Zechariah, and Simeon—by all accounts ordinary people living ordinary lives of faith—stand out to us as prophets, speaking the Word of God in the power of God.

Simeon, we are told, was promised by God that he would not die until he had seen the Messiah with his own eyes. As a young man, this must have been an exciting prospect. This promise must have comforted Simeon when he looked around and saw how much the world, and Israel, in particular, needed the salvation of God. But as he grew older, the knowledge may have begun to wear on him as he wondered how long he would have live to see the promise fulfilled. It is with great relief that Simeon finds Mary and Joseph and the baby in the temple and recognizes the child as the Messiah of God, for he knows that God has released him from his waiting.

To be a prophet is to see things clearly and from God's point of view. It is a calling that none of the prophets welcomed: each of the Old Testament prophets testifies to the disruption of his life by God's call, and all of the hardship he suffers. The way he sees the world, and the words God gives him are welcomed by almost no one. The New Testament prophets are in much the same situation: Zechariah and Elizabeth understand what will be required of their son. Simeon, with great clarity of vision, recognizes what Jesus' identity as Messiah will cost Mary. To be a prophet is to see all the pain as well as the joy.

We would rather not see the world most of the time. We especially do not want to see it as God sees it, with all of its pain and sin and death. And yet we are those who pray with some regularity that God's "kingdom come on earth as it is in heaven." Like Elizabeth and Zechariah and Simeon we pray for change, we pray to see the day when Christ comes; and like them, the Holy Spirit fills us. The age of prophecy is not past, and God still calls us to speak as prophets to the current age, to declare that salvation has come and that the kingdom is coming. We have models of ordinary people who learned how to sing the message, just as God is trying to teach us to sing, and just as we will sing when moved by the Holy Spirit.

> *O Lord, we are not sure we want to be prophets to this present age. It would be easier to close our eyes and ears and mouths and be content with our own place in heaven. Nevertheless, we pray that your Holy Spirit will fill us, that you will teach us to sing, and that we will be able to sing out the message of salvation, even as your prophet Simeon did. In the name and the power of Jesus Christ we pray. Amen.*

_____Friday_____
Simeon's Proclamation

Scripture: Luke 2:31-32

Simeon is the first—but not the last—to sing the song to those outside of Israel. The coming of the Messiah has always been understood as a promise *to* Israel *for* Israel, and most understood that the salvation God would bring through the Messiah was to be a saving of the nation and its people. This was not to be salvation for anyone else, not a message for those outside of the Chosen People with whom God had dealt for so long. Even after Easter and the Day of Pentecost, the apostles would have some heated arguments over whether the gospel was for the Jews only or could be taken to those outside of Israel as well.

Simeon very simply proclaims that this small Messiah whom he holds in his arms, there in the temple court, is for "all peoples, a light for revelation to the Gentiles and for glory to your people Israel." This is not revolutionary—the prophets of the Old Testament scriptures proclaimed that the day would come when the whole world would turn to the God of Israel and join in worshiping the Lord. It is a reminder to those who would limit the work of God to something less than the whole of creation that God will not be limited. If Israel is the Chosen People, those outside of Israel are no less the concern of the God who created us all. The Messiah will draw the Gentiles—all of the non-Jewish world—to God.

This is a powerful message because there are many ways we limit God's concern and message, holding it for ourselves and excluding those who are outside our circle. We often speak and act as if God is the God of the United

States. We will share God with others, but God still belongs to us and will favor us over everyone else. The Messiah comes to all the nations, even those who do not recognize him and do not follow him now. God is the God of us all, even if there are some who are determined to deny it. Like Israel, our task is not to keep God to ourselves but to serve as a lampstand, holding God up for all the world to see that they might come to the Lord. This is not easy. To be a lampstand means to have the light of God constantly shining on us and showing everything we do. There are those who will criticize us for not practicing what we preach. But our glory will be in bringing all the world to the God and the Father of our Lord Jesus Christ.

> *O Lord, God of the universe, help us to remember that once we were outside of Israel, but that we have been adopted into the Promise by your great love. Remind us that to be a Chosen People means that we have more responsibility for the rest of the peoples of the world, not less. Use us to reach out to all of your children in all of the world, as we are all brothers and sisters of Jesus, in whose name we pray. Amen.*

_____Christmas Eve_____
The Angels' Song

Scripture: Luke 2:10-12

The shepherds were terrified by the appearance of the angel in the sky near Bethlehem, and well they might be! We have tamed the angels—made them just like us with wings and white robes and haloes—and so have lost the awesome magnificence of those creatures who are sent to speak for God. But the appearance of a genuine angel, a real messenger of the Almighty God, is terrifying. Both Isaiah and John the Evangelist testify that the angels are different creatures than any on earth, alive with flame and smoke, and with voices that rock the very foundations of heaven. It is no wonder that when they appear to human beings, they carry the fearsome aspect of those who stand constantly in the presence of the Living God, glowing with God's holiness and power as they deliver God's message. No wonder people are reported to faint when angels appear to them!

We have also tamed the message. The angels come to the shepherds with the most important word that has ever been spoken to humankind: the Savior has been born. This is not to be taken lightly. It marks the end of God's relationship with the creation and with the Chosen People as it had been from the beginning to this moment; everything will now be different—*every* thing. God has turned the world upside down, and the angels are telling the shepherds in the fields. Why not Herod or Caesar? Why not the chief priest of the temple, or the leaders of the Sanhedrin? The Word of God *now* belongs to the common working people and not to the rich or the powerful. Why in Bethlehem in a stable instead of a

palace in Jerusalem or Rome or Athens or Alexandria?
God *now* dwells with the lowly and the oppressed and
the homeless. The world has been turned upside down!

It is a moment like this that we await when we look
for the return of Christ, a moment when God will turn
the world upside down and reorder everything. The
angels probably will not come to Rome or New York or
Nashville; they will not come to church leaders or
bishops or clergy. When the angels sing again, they will
go to the field, to the rural community, to proclaim the
good news that God is in charge, that salvation has come,
and that all is right with the (upside down) world.

*O Lord our God, in the stillness, the beauty, the
splendor of this night, grant that we may rejoice in
having the world turned upside down, in having the
Holy come to dwell in the midst of us. Give us ears
for the song of the angels, that we may grasp the
importance of the news that salvation has come to
the earth and its peoples. And then give us voices to
sing out the good news to all who will hear and to
all who will not hear, that they may hear it one day.
In the name of the Babe of Bethlehem we pray.
Amen.*

Christmas Day
The Glory of Christmas

Scripture: Luke 2:13-14

The last word of the angels, the last word of these songs of Advent, is the word of praise to God. All that the prophets, the angels, and those filled with the Holy Spirit have spoken and sung comes together in this brief hymn: "Glory to God in the highest heaven!" It is all for the glory of God: every word, every prayer, every act of faith and devotion, every act of obedience. Our attention is focused back where it belongs: on God.

These days of Advent have been busy days, full of distractions, many times leaving us exhausted and frustrated. Today it is here: Christmas has come, whether we were ready or not. And the glory of Christmas does not lie in whether we were ready or not, but in the glory of God that poured into the world through the birth of the Christ, glory that continues to pour out upon us in the presence and work of the Holy Spirit, glory that will be fully revealed to us on the day when Christ returns. It is time for us to lay down the shopping lists and wrapping paper, the cookie sheets and oven timer, and take up the song of praise that the angels began: "Glory to God in the highest heaven." This is, after all, what this day is all about. This is all that we have to do: to join in the angels' song.

Today begins the celebration of the coming of God into the world. Advent is over. Christmas has just begun, and it will not be over until the wise men arrive from the East on January 6. We have sung the songs of Advent; now it is time to sing the songs of Christmas, to rejoice over the birth of Jesus in Bethlehem. Do not put

Christmas away too soon—keep the joy and the song going for the whole season. We have put too much effort into getting ready to celebrate for just one day. One day cannot contain all the joy of the good news that has come to us.

> *Almighty and Everlasting God, we rejoice in this day of your coming to us. Bless this holy season that we may sing the songs with joy, tell the story with gladness, and carry the news with us always and everywhere that God, the Creator of heaven and earth, has come to save the world and that all the earth is called to rejoice. In the name of Jesus Christ, who has come and will come again, we pray. Amen and amen.*

*****Notes and Reflections from Week Four*****

_____About the Author_____

The Reverend Mary Anna Vidakovich is a United Methodist pastor and has served both Huey and Beckemeyer United Methodist churches in Illinois (Clinton County) since 1990. Prior to that she was the pastor of Bethel and Kane United Methodist Churches in Dow and Kane, Illinois.

The author is a native of Tucson, Arizona and has pastored churches in Southern Illinois since 1980. She currently serves on the Annual Conference Board of Church and Society as vice chairperson for Peace with Justice, and on the Vandalia District Committee on Ordained Ministry. She holds degrees from the University of the Pacific (Bachelor of Arts) in Stockton, California; and Saint Paul School of Theology (Master of Divinity) in Kansas City, Missouri. Also, she attended St. John's College in Santa Fe, New Mexico.

Reverend Vidakovich enjoys needlework, drawing, and quilting. She is married to John, who is also a United Methodist pastor. They have three children: Joel, Petra, and Hannah.